Henry Johnson AND Harlem's Own

Jacqueline Maloy

GReaT S#uRCe®
EDUCATION GROUP
A Division of Houghton Mifflin Company

Reading Advantage Authors
Laura Robb
James F. Baumann
Carol J. Fuhler
Joan Kindig

Project Manager
Ellen Sternhell

Editor
Jeri Cipriano

Design and Production
Preface, Inc.

Photography and Illustration
Front cover, pp. 25, 34, 45 © Corbis; pp. 1, 6, 11, 14, 18, 30, 32, 35, 42, 49, 51, 58 © Bettmann/Corbis; p. 9 map art by Precision Graphics; p. 16 © Elizabeth R. Hibbs/Hulton Archive/Getty Images; pp. 21–22 map art by Sue Carlson; p. 37 © Hulton Archive/Getty Images; p. 39 courtesy of Reflections of Asia; pp. 52, 54 © National Archives and Records Administration; p. 55 courtesy of Albany County Convention & Visitors Bureau; p. 56 © AP Photo/Dennis Cook; p. 59 courtesy of New York State Museum

Printed in the United States of America

International Standard Book Number: 0-669-51408-X

2 3 4 5 6 7 8 9 10 – RRDC – 09 08 07 06 05

CONTENTS

Introduction

Setting the Stage

More than likely, Henry Johnson is not a familiar name. That's partly because your study of history has not focused on World War I. You mostly have been learning about events that took place long before Henry Johnson ever appeared on Earth and fought in World War I. In addition, World War I (1914–1918), also called the Great War, has not been the subject of as many war movies as other wars in history. So you probably haven't seen this war played out on the big screen.

World War I, however, was indeed a great war. It involved most of the world's great powers. And it was one of the bloodiest wars in history. The war included assassinations, grueling land battles, submarine warfare, ship and airplane attacks, and attacks involving poison gas. According to the facts, sixty-five million men served in the armies of numerous countries. About nine million people were killed. About twenty million people were wounded. The treaties that ended the war changed much of Europe and the Middle East geographically and politically.

Why Henry Johnson and Harlem's Own?

Henry Johnson

In any war, there are stories of great courage and heroism. World War I was no exception. The story of Henry Johnson and the regiment (unit) he fought with in World War I is important because their story is a mix of so many things. There was controversy, creativity, bravery, tragedy, and triumph. The regiment was referred to as Harlem's Own because many of the men came from Harlem, New York. They were also called the Black Rattlers. The Germans gave them the name Hell Fighters. As African Americans, they had to fight for the right to be American soldiers. They turned out to be extraordinary ones.

Henry Johnson himself and the regiment as a whole were all war heroes. And, most unusual but true, some of them who were musicians also became known as a band. They recorded music while they were soldiers! As you read about these individuals and the war, you will understand why the men were honored with medals and why they should be remembered.

CHAPTER

1

Before World War I

In Europe

In the late 1800s and into the early 1900s, there was a strong spirit of nationalism in countries all over Europe. *Nationalism* is a fierce pride in one's country. As part of this pride, European countries wanted to expand their power and their wealth. To do this, they needed to take control over more land in Europe and other parts of the world.

Several European countries already had colonies in other places. But this was not enough. These countries wanted more power and more land. So, they built strong armies and threatened to use force to get what they wanted. (Using big armies as a threat of force to gain power is called *militarism*.)

The leaders of the European countries did not trust one another. To protect their nations, they formed alliances. An *alliance* is an agreement between countries. Members of an alliance would help a country fight if it was attacked by an enemy. This was a way to maintain the balance of power. Europe's leaders did not want to see any one nation become too dominant.

By 1907, there were two opposing sides in Europe. Great Britain, France, Russia, and Japan were on one side. They were the Allies, or Allied Powers. Serbia also became part of the Allies. Germany, Austria-Hungary, Italy, Bulgaria, and the Ottoman Empire (part of where Turkey is today) were on the other side. They were the Central Powers. Italy left the Central Powers later in the war and joined the Allied Powers. In the end, thirty-two countries became part of the Allied Powers.

Germany was determined to become *the* main power on the continent of Europe. The Germans also intended to challenge the superiority of Great Britain's navy. These factors were part of the mix that led to the development of the Great War.

Europe before World War I

Most European countries were either with the Allied Powers or Central Powers. However, some countries remained neutral—not on either side.

In the United States

Many things were happening in the United States during the same period before World War I. The United States was growing both in land and in population. More states were added, and many people came as immigrants from other countries to live in the United States. People were moving to the United States from all over the world.

In 1898, the United States fought a war with Spain to help free Cuba from Spanish rule. It was called the Spanish-American War. The war lasted only a few months, between April and August. In the end, Spain granted Cuba its freedom and gave up Guam, Puerto Rico, and the Philippine Islands to the United States.

Back in the United States, in the late 1800s and into the early 1900s, people's everyday lives differed, depending on where they lived. In the North, there was a lot of growth in industry. More jobs became available. People from every background and race lived and worked together. It was not always friendly, but it was a lot better than in the South.

After the Civil War ended in 1865, the South went through many years of reconstruction. African Americans were free from the bonds of slavery, but the former slaves had to build completely new lives.

It was not easy because white voters passed laws in states throughout the South that deprived African Americans of their civil rights, such as personal freedom and equal treatment. The laws defined blacks as inferior to whites.

Two Civil Rights Acts (1866 and 1875) and Enforcement Acts (1870s) prevented white people in the South from officially depriving blacks of their civil rights. But there still was segregation between black and white Americans in most areas of life. Marriage between African Americans and white Americans was outlawed. African Americans had to go to different schools from white people. They had to use different stores and different public bathrooms.

Unfortunately, segregation continued well into the first part of the twentieth century.

Most black people were very poor because there were no jobs for them. A lot of blacks worked for tobacco companies or factories that made cloth. But it was a "hand-to-mouth life" with not much hope for improvement.

The Great Migration

Starting around 1900, there was a huge migration, or movement, of African Americans from the South to the North. Thousands and thousands of African Americans moved to northern cities to escape the problems of racism, to get jobs, and to have a better life. Cities such as Chicago, Detroit, New York, and Cleveland had some of the biggest increases in population. There were plenty of jobs in factories, on railroads, and in many other places. Some railroad companies even paid African Americans' travel expenses to the North.

The challenges of living in a city environment were quite big for many of the new African American city dwellers. Nevertheless, a stream of migrants from the South continued into the 1940s. The first large, urban, black communities in the North developed especially between 1910 and 1930.

So now it's time to meet Henry Johnson, who came into the world of the South almost at the end of the 1800s. As already mentioned, it was a world of segregation and poverty for African Americans. It was a world from which Johnson felt he eventually had to escape.

CHAPTER
2
Meet Henry Johnson

Henry Johnson lived an ordinary life before he became an extraordinary hero.

Winston-Salem, North Carolina

Henry Johnson was born in 1897 in Winston-Salem, North Carolina. At the time, no one guessed that he would grow up to become a famous war hero. It was President Theodore Roosevelt, who wrote a book about World War I and named Henry Johnson as one of the war's five greatest heroes.

According to Roosevelt's book, Johnson's parents were poor. As African Americans, they lived lives segregated from white people. Actually, during the 1890s in Winston-Salem, white people and black people *did* come together sometimes at musical events and baseball games. But by the 1900s, even that had changed.

Just a few years after Henry Johnson was born, voting laws changed in North Carolina. These laws made it nearly impossible for African Americans and poor white people to vote. Things seemed to be getting worse instead of better for African Americans throughout the South.

As part of the Great Migration, Johnson's family moved to the North when Johnson was still quite young. They moved to Albany, New York.

Albany, New York

Things were different for African Americans in New York state. They still had a hard time getting top jobs, but segregation was not the law in New York. At that time in the city of Albany, there was a small population of African Americans. White and black Americans lived in mixed neighborhoods. The schools and churches were also mixed. Voters passed laws against segregation, and black men could vote.

Life in New York was a little easier. People were more accepting of each other.

As a young man in Albany, Henry did find jobs. He spent some time working in a coal yard. He also worked at a pharmacy mixing soda. Mostly, he worked as a baggage handler at the Albany train station.

Henry had other good luck in Albany, too. He met his future wife, Cornelia Jackson, at a church in the area. They married and lived downtown at 23 Monroe Street. That was near his job at the train station. Italian Americans who were new to the country and African Americans lived in this mixed neighborhood.

Johnson took part in his community. He was a member of a church. He also belonged to a community group of African Americans.

According to Johnson's son Herman, his father had a great sense of humor and people liked him. He was small—he stood at just five feet four inches and weighed one hundred thirty pounds. No one took special notice of him then.

Things seemed to be going well for Henry in Albany. In the rest of the world, though, young men from many European countries were going to war.

3

The Start of the Great War

The Assassinations

The event that started World War I, sending many young men into battle, began in an area in south-eastern Europe. On June 28, 1914, a young Serbian nationalist shot Archduke Franz Ferdinand and his wife, Sophie. The archduke was one day supposed to become the emperor of the Austro-Hungarian Empire.

Serbia was an independent country that wanted control of Bosnia and Herzogovina. These nearby places to Serbia were ruled by Austria-Hungary. To change the situation, the Serbians chose to assassinate the archduke and his wife. Then, they could try to take control.

Archduke Franz Ferdinand with his wife, Sophie

Although not all Serbians were involved in the assassination, the leaders of Austria-Hungary didn't care. First, they killed hundreds of Serbs. Then, they declared war on the whole nation of Serbia. Russia immediately sided with Serbia against Austria-Hungary because Serbia was already a part of the Allied Powers.

As explained in Chapter 1, Germany and Austria-Hungary were already on the same side —part of the Central Powers. So, it was clear that Germany would support Austria-Hungary. Now, there were Russia and its allies on one side and Germany and its allies on the other. The conflict spread and erupted into a world war.

In August 1914, Germany declared war on Russia. Since France was part of the Allies, Germany declared war on France, too. England declared war on Germany, and so it went on . . .

Many countries were at war, but the United States tried to stay out of it. Still, more people in the United States sympathized with the Allies than with the Central Powers. The United States thought that Germany was trying to get too much territory and power. As time went on, it became difficult for Americans to stay neutral.

Why America Joined the Allies

The United States had used submarines as far back as the Revolutionary War. However, it was the Germans in World War I that made submarines truly powerful weapons of war. Submarines were often called U-boats, short for underwater boats.

Throughout the war, Germany used submarines to block supplies from getting to Great Britain. The submarines torpedoed boats carrying these supplies. Sometimes, though, the German subs hit boats that had nothing to do with the war.

In 1915, German U-boats hit a United States oil tanker. Germany said it was an accident. The Germans offered to pay for the ship. But less than a week later, an U-boat hit a British passenger ship, the *Lusitania*. Of the 1,198 people who were killed, 128 were Americans.

Americans were outraged. At first, the Germans promised not to torpedo anymore ships from countries that weren't in the war. Months later, the Germans changed their minds. They warned that they would attack any merchant ship that headed toward Great Britain. The Germans sunk four American ships, so America went to war.

The Eastern Front

Most of the fighting took place in two areas called the Fronts. Men at the Fronts were at the front line of the action, where combat took place. On the Eastern Front, Germany and Russia fought in the Russian Empire.

The Western Front

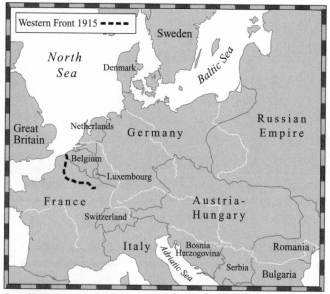

On the Western Front, men fought in the trenches in Belgium and Northern France. There, Great Britain, France, and the United States battled the invading troops of the Central Powers.

America at War

By the time America joined the Allies in the war in 1917, fighting had been going on for a few years. Both sides had hoped the war would be short. Both sides were disappointed.

The Allies badly needed the United States to join the fight. Thousands of men from Great Britain, France, Italy, and Russia had already been killed.

Young men from all over the world fought the battles of the Great War. Henry Johnson and other African Americans volunteered to become part of the fight.

CHAPTER

4

Henry Johnson and Harlem's Own Enter WWI

The Fifteenth Infantry Regiment of New York

Henry Johnson joined the army on June 15, 1917. He and a few of his friends volunteered in New York City. They joined the Fifteenth Infantry Regiment of the New York National Guard. Except for the officers, this regiment was made up of African American men. In those days, many American military people thought that black people should be separate from white people.

A lot of the men in the unit came from an area in New York City called Harlem. People called the whole regiment "Harlem's Own." By the end of the war, the Germans had a new name to call them.

In addition to being called Harlem's Own, the men of the Fifteenth Infantry Regiment of the New York National Guard had another name for themselves—the Black Rattlers.

Some white people didn't think that black men should fight in a war. About 368,000 black men joined the army in World War I. Only about one in ten of them actually saw combat.

A lot of people knew that it was silly to keep African Americans from serving their country. In New York, some men had worked hard on the issue. They wanted African Americans to have their own National Guard unit. One of these men was Colonel William Hayward.

A lot of people already knew Colonel Hayward. He had fought in the Spanish-American War in 1898. He was a good leader. After helping to organize the Fifteenth Regiment, Colonel Hayward became its leader.

Colonel Hayward believed strongly in his men. He wanted to make sure that the regiment was treated fairly. He asked if his regiment could join the famous "Rainbow Division" of the National Guard units. The answer was *no*. Black, they told him, was not a color of the rainbow.

The Rainbow Division was made up of National Guard units from twenty-six states and Washington, D.C. This was done so that states wouldn't compete with each other for the honor of being the first to send their National Guard units to Europe. There were certainly people of different backgrounds in those units. The whole idea was to be fair, although it really wasn't.

The name Rainbow Division came from a statement that said, "the 42nd Division stretches like a rainbow from one end of America to the other." The division became the 42nd Infantry Division. It was organized in September 1917.

Not being able to join the Rainbow Division made all of the men in the Fifteenth Regiment even more determined to prove their abilities. They wanted to show that a black man could fight just as well as any white man.

It wasn't easy for the Fifteenth. They trained by marching through Harlem. They used the second floor of a theater for some "gun" practice. They didn't even have guns, so they had to use broomsticks.

Colonel Hayward had a hard time getting supplies for his unit. He had trouble getting guns. Then he found out that the army was giving guns to private gun clubs. Colonel Hayward had members of the unit write letters asking for guns for their "gun clubs." That's how he finally got rifles for his unit.

Training for War

The Fifteenth Regiment left New York City to get field training in Peekskill, New York. Peekskill is upstate about an hour from New York City. Most of the men had never been in a military camp before. They drilled and practiced with their rifles from morning until night. They also learned how to perform guard duty. That training later helped them both in the United States and in France.

After that, the Fifteenth trained near Poughkeepsie, New York. There, the men had to get used to one of the common enemies of any soldier—lice. When these bugs came, they had to soak their clothes in gasoline to get rid of them.

After five weeks, training was over. Orders came for the Fifteenth. The orders said that the men needed to guard important places in the United States. This group of two thousand men was split into smaller groups. They went to fifty different areas in New York, New Jersey, and Pennsylvania.

The men knew what they were doing. For almost two months, they were on duty at train stations, ports, and in major cities. Henry Johnson did guard duty in Albany and Rotterdam, both in New York. No property was destroyed while the men of the Fifteenth stood guard. And they even caught a German spy!

Still, this was not what the men had signed up for. They wanted to go to Europe. They wanted to fight in the Great War.

Finally, new orders came. The men were to go south to get ready to fight in the war. They went to Spartanburg, South Carolina.

Trouble in Spartanburg

It wasn't easy for the men to train in Spartanburg. Some white people there did not like the idea of "colored," or black, men coming from the North. Spartanburg still had separate stores and public bathrooms for African Americans. This was just like Winston-Salem, North Carolina, where Henry Johnson had been born.

One city official told a reporter from the *New York Times*, " . . . if any of those colored soldiers go in any of our soda stores and . . . ask to be served, they'll be knocked down. Somebody will throw a bottle. We don't allow negroes to use the same glass that a white man may later drink out of."

The men in the Fifteenth had no intentions of stirring up any trouble. All they wanted to do was train. In their spare time, they enjoyed playing and listening to music. Some of the people in the Fifteenth had been singers and musicians before they joined the regiment. These men used their musical talents and became the unit's entertainers. But some racial situations did flare up. Before things got too out of control, however, the Fifteenth got their orders to go to France.

The regiment's musicians played for the troops and citizens in many places in France. The band became known as the Hell Fighters Band. Its leader was James Reese Europe.

The Long Journey to France

The men of the Fifteenth were excited about going to France. In October, they set out from New York on a ship called the *Pocahontas*. It wasn't exactly smooth sailing, though. After two days at sea, the ship broke down. They all had to go back to port. The men stayed at Camp Merritt in New Jersey.

During those weeks, it was hard to keep the men at the camp since they were so close to home. They wanted to see their families. The officers had to work with the police to keep the men where they needed to be.

On November 12, the Fifteenth left for France again. This time, their ship caught fire. They had to go back to port again. But they stayed onboard until the ship was fixed. It took four weeks.

On December 11, the ship started out once more. On December 12, an oil tanker crashed into it. The men didn't want to go back to port this time. Luckily, a company of expert mechanics was on the ship. They did the repairs themselves. The ship kept on its way, although the accident had put a big hole in the side of the ship.

As they crossed the ocean, the men had to worry about submarine attacks. Submarines were hard to detect and avoid. Sometimes, there were drills for the men to practice getting off the boat. It was hard to tell whether the drills were practice or if they were really being attacked.

During the long nights on the ship, Henry Johnson and his friends must have wondered what they had signed up for. Luckily, their ship made the journey safely across the dangerous waters. On December 27, 1917, the men landed at Brest, France.

Ships traveled in convoys across the ocean. The convoys were groups of ships traveling together, making the trip safer for everyone.

CHAPTER
5
The Battlefront in France

The 15th Regiment Becomes the 369th

The troops, or soldiers, of the Fifteenth N.Y. Regiment (also referred to as the 15th) thought that they would be sent into battle right after they landed in France. However, they were moved to a place called St. Nazaire. There, the men were put to work as laborers. They spent time building a railroad yard, repairing roads, and unloading ships. The men kept asking their officers, "When do we get to fight?"

The men thought that they would have a chance when they were sent to another place, Colquidan. That was an artillery camp, a place with large weapons, and a prisoner-of-war camp. But it was not the case at first. The men's orders were to guard German prisoners.

While the men guarded the prisoners of war, their leader, Colonel Hayward, spoke to General John J. Pershing. He was the commander of the big American force of troops. Colonel Hayward tried to convince General Pershing to let the 15th become part of the big American Expeditionary Force. But the general would not consider the idea of an all-black regiment in his army.

General Pershing did, however, make a compromise. He attached the 15th Regiment to the French high command and changed the 15th's name to the 369th U.S. Infantry. The regiment was an American unit, but they got their orders from French officers.

The 369th spent the next few weeks training in a foreign army. The focus was on grenade throwing and bayonet work. A *bayonet* is a kind of large knife that is attached to the front of a rifle and used for stabbing or slashing in hand-to-hand fighting. The men also learned the French language.

bayonet

Trench Warfare

By May of 1918, the 369th was learning trench warfare among French units at the Western Front. A *trench* is a long, narrow ditch in the ground with the soil piled up on one or both sides. Soldiers used the trenches to protect themselves during combat.

The men of the 369th wore French helmets and used French rifles at the front.

The men on both sides of the battle actually lived for weeks or even months at a time in the trenches that were dug all along the Western Front.

Life in the trenches was horrible. One constant problem was rats. Captain Hamilton Fish, Jr., wrote that there were rats of "all sizes [that] eat up everything in smelling distance. They eat through the men's pockets . . . climb over them at night and are generally a pest."

Rats weren't the only problem. The trenches were cold and damp. Men often kept their shoes on all of the time they lived in trenches. Sometimes these soldiers would then develop *trench foot*. When men stood in their wet shoes for a long time, their feet would become numb. Sometimes, they would get infected. In the worst cases, gangrene would set in. Then, the toes or even a whole foot would have to be amputated, or cut off.

The Allies and the Central Powers both had trenches that ran across from each other for nearly five hundred miles. The trenches were pretty close to one another. In fact, they were so close that the enemies could see one another's trenches. The men called the space between the trenches "no man's land."

There were soldiers on all sides of the trenches to protect the men. There were also guards who listened so that they could alert their unit if they heard enemies moving toward their side.

Men who were serving as guards for the trenches had to stand in outposts. These listening posts were right at the edge of no man's land. That meant that soldiers doing guard duty didn't have anyone to protect *them*.

In no man's land, men from both sides put up lots of barbed wire. The barbed wire blocked enemies who might otherwise charge quickly into the trenches. When soldiers wanted to attack, they had to cut through barbed wire first.

The First American Heroes of the War

In the early hours of May 14, Henry Johnson had guard duty, along with Needham Roberts. Needham Roberts, from Trenton, New Jersey, had volunteered for the U.S. Army as soon as the United States declared war. In fact, at nineteen years old, he had sneaked away from his parents' home to do it!

Johnson and Roberts were at an outpost in the Argonne Forest in France. They had originally been part of a group of five who were on guard all night watching for the enemy. Since it had been quiet for a night and a day, three of the men left Johnson and Roberts the following night to go into a nearby trench to get some rest.

While on duty, Roberts thought he heard some barbed wire being cut. He crawled over to Johnson and they both listened. They couldn't see anything, but the sound told them that someone was out there.

Roberts and Johnson shouted for the corporal of the guard. Then, they threw a rocket to light the area. All at once, more than twenty Germans attacked. They were shooting rifles and throwing grenades. Roberts got hit right away. He was badly wounded and couldn't get up to fight.

The German grenade attack kept the three men in the nearby trench from doing anything. So, Henry Johnson was left to fight the German patrol on his own!

Henry Johnson didn't hesitate. He fired three shots at the German attackers. The first two missed their mark. The third bullet struck and killed an enemy soldier just as he was coming over the rim of the trench.

At that point, Johnson realized he was out of bullets. That didn't stop him. He used the end of his rifle like a baseball bat to clobber another German.

By then, Johnson had his own bullet wounds. But when he saw two enemy soldiers trying to carry Needham Roberts away, he went after one with a bolo knife. Johnson stabbed the top of the German's head.

Johnson used a bolo knife like this one to fight the Germans.

While Johnson was removing his knife from the German's head, Johnson had another surprise. The German whom Johnson had clobbered with the rifle had recovered and came rushing at Johnson. The German shot Johnson in the right forearm, right hip, and left leg. But that still didn't stop Johnson! With whatever he had left in him, Johnson stabbed the German hard in the stomach. That was the end of the German.

There were still more German attackers, however. Roberts couldn't do much because of his injuries. But he was able to hand grenades to Johnson, who threw them at the Germans. Finally, after a fierce battle that lasted an hour, the Germans ran. In that time, Johnson had killed four men. He and Roberts wounded many more.

Once the fighting was over, Johnson and Roberts were left wounded in the outpost. Some say Roberts and Johnson were singing when the relief party came. Others say that Johnson was barely conscious and whispering, "Corporal of the guard, corporal of the guard . . ." Most likely, Johnson fainted from shock after the battle. Both Henry Johnson and Needham Roberts had to go to a field hospital to recover from their wounds. Both were wounded for life.

Just after "The Battle of Henry Johnson" took place, three American war correspondents were looking for a story. They decided to visit the 369th to see the African American soldiers in action.

Two of the men wrote for newspapers. Their stories appeared back in the United States within a few days. Another man, Irving Cobb, wrote for the *Saturday Evening Post*, which was a popular monthly magazine. Because of the stories that these men wrote, the heroism of Henry Johnson and Needham Roberts became national news. Some said that Henry Johnson was America's first true hero of the war.

It wasn't only those in the United States who were impressed. The French Army honored both Johnson and Roberts with a special award—the Croix de Guerre (KWAH du GARE). This is the French War Cross. The Croix de Guerre is a very high military honor. Johnson got the Croix de Guerre with gold leaf—an even higher honor. Johnson and Roberts were the first American soldiers of any race to receive this award in World War I.

Henry Johnson received the Croix de Guerre. It is France's highest honor for battlefield bravery.

Needham Roberts also received France's Croix de Guerre.

CHAPTER
6
The Final Months of War

Bastille Day

Henry Johnson spent three months in the hospital. For nearly all of this time, the 369th was still fighting. "Harlem's Own" spent a total of 191 days in combat. That was longer than any other American regiment.

Though the war already seemed endless, these men had more battles in store. In the summer of 1918, Germany tried to launch a major attack. They chose July 14, France's Bastille Day, to strike. Bastille Day honors one of the important days of the French Revolution. The Germans believed that July 14 was a perfect day to attack because everyone would be celebrating the holiday.

Luckily for the Allies, a German prisoner explained the German plan. The Allies made their own plan and tricked the Germans.

As soon as they knew the attack had started, the Allies got most of their soldiers out of the frontline trenches. A few men stayed so that the Germans would not realize what was going on. These brave soldiers had a very dangerous job.

Some of the men who stayed in the frontline were from the 369th. These few men had to throw grenades and fire rifles as quickly as they could. They had to seem like a much bigger force.

The trick worked. Germany attacked, and most of the Allies pulled back. Amazingly, the sixteen men of the 369th who stayed in the frontline trenches all survived the German shelling.

Thinking that the Allies had retreated, the Germans advanced past the frontline. The Allied soldiers who were left in the rear trenches threw signal rockets. (Rear trenches were sets of trenches behind the frontline trench.) Then the Allies struck back, hard, and the Germans had to retreat. This would be the last time the Germans launched a major attack on the Western Front.

During their 191 days in combat, the 369th never lost any ground. None of the men was ever taken prisoner.

The Battle of the Meuse-Argonne

Everyone wanted the war to end. France, Great Britain, Russia, and Germany had lost many of their best young men in the four years of terrible warfare. Some of those who lived had lost arms or legs. Some were "shell-shocked." The term *shell-shocked* refers to men whose minds were destroyed by the horror of war. Some never recovered.

The Allies and Central Powers had lost so much already, but neither side was willing to compromise much. The sacrifice of so many young men had to mean something, they believed. Certainly, no country wanted to give up any land.

Allied forces knew that they had an advantage because the numbers were on their side. Although they had lost hundreds of thousands of men in battle, they had also gained hundreds of thousands of soldiers every month. That was because America had joined the war. The German forces had lost hundreds of thousands of men who couldn't be replaced. The Germans had to pull in fourteen-year-old boys to fight.

Germany was in trouble. Austria-Hungary was weak. So, the Allies decided to beat back the forces of the Central Powers in one great push.

The 369th was to be part of the push. The idea was to have over one million of the Allied soldiers move to attack the Germans in the Argonne Forest. The Germans had held this land since the first year of the war.

On September 26, 1918, the attack began. On the first day, thousands of Germans surrendered. It looked like the battle might easily be won. It was not.

The three battalions from the 369th suffered awful losses. Its Third Battalion began with about seven hundred men and twenty officers. After one day, this battalion was down to just one hundred fifty men and seven officers. After fighting in terrifying conditions for nine days straight, the Second and First Battalions had also lost about one-third of their men and officers.

Still, the Third Battalion captured one hundred and twenty-five prisoners. The men also gained valuable land. They helped to take Sechault, an important railroad junction. For that, France awarded the entire 369th the Croix de Guerre.

During the war, the Germans called this regiment "bloodthirsty black men." The Germans also gave them the nickname "Hell Fighters."

Whatever name the 369th was called really didn't matter. What the regiment did during the time they were in France absolutely did matter. They were the first Americans, black or white, to reach the combat zone in France. They were the first to cross the Rhine River in the offensive against the Germans. They were continuously in combat for 191 days, which was longer than any other American unit.

Armistice

On the eleventh hour of November 11, 1918, an armistice, or truce, was signed. Finally, the war was over. It had been the worst war in the history of the world at that point in time. In addition to the millions who died fighting in World War I, millions of civilians died from starvation, disease, and bombs.

In January 1919, the Allied nations met near Paris, France. They had to decide what would happen next, now that the war was over. The meeting became known as the Paris Peace Conference.

At the conference, the Allied Powers worked out an agreement. It was called the Treaty of Versailles (vehr SIGH). The Allies decided that Germany should pay for the war since this nation had started it.

The men sitting are the Allied leaders at the Paris Peace Conference. The man at the far right is U.S. President Woodrow Wilson.

Germany lost territory. Germany also had to pay money to the Allies and agree not to make tanks, military airplanes, big weapons, or submarines.

It was hoped that the conditions listed in the agreement would prevent Germany from ever becoming powerful enough again to make war. (Of course, this was not the case. Twenty years or so later, World War II would begin with Germany as the key player again.)

The cost of the war for everyone involved was extremely high. Deaths and injuries of soldiers and civilians were in the millions. The financial loss was enormous, too. It was estimated that the total cost of the war was more than three hundred billion dollars. That was a huge amount of money for that time.

7

Coming Home

A New York City Welcome

On February 12, 1919, the 369th finally came
home. A few days later, they marched in a parade
in New York City. Most of the other African
American regiments were not welcomed home
with any great fuss. But New York hailed the
369th as heroes.

**Almost a million people came to welcome "Harlem's
Own" back home to New York.**

The soldiers paraded in front of a huge crowd, including Governor Al Smith. Everyone cheered for Harlem's Own. The crowd was so loud that it was hard to hear the band.

During the homecoming parade for the 369th, Henry Johnson smiled the whole way up to Harlem.

Henry Johnson: Veteran

Henry Johnson was famous in New York City and in Albany, New York. Advertisers used his picture to sell war bonds and war stamps. One advertisement said, "Henry Johnson licked a dozen Germans. How many stamps have you licked today?"

Oddly, though, the United States didn't give Johnson any medals during those years—not even a Purple Heart, our medal for bravery in action. And, even though Johnson had received almost twenty wounds, he got no disability pay.

While Johnson enjoyed his fame, he had a hard time after the war. It was difficult for him to work because of all of his injuries. His father-in-law was a minister, and he was quite a strict man. He didn't like it that Henry played the piano and drank whiskey in bars. After a while, Henry and his wife Cornelia separated. She raised their three children.

Henry Johnson's son Herman got to see Henry sometimes during the summers. He remembers that his father, like many veterans, never talked about the war or his heroism. In fact, Herman said, "You would have had to hogtie him to get him to talk about the war."

Henry Johnson's fame faded as people went on with their lives after the war. He died a poor man just a decade after the parade that had welcomed him home. He was buried with other war heroes at Arlington National Cemetery in Virginia.

Johnson and the rest of Harlem's Own are not forgotten, though. Recordings of the band music that the musicians of the regiment played are still available. As mentioned earlier, the band had become known as the Hell Fighters band.

Remember that the members of the Hell Fighters Band were soldiers first. But they did perform all over France when they were not in combat.

Today, Albany, New York, celebrates Henry Johnson. People drive down Henry Johnson Boulevard. They can visit a bronze statue of Johnson in Washington Park. There is also a building named after Johnson and a mural honoring his heroism.

Decades after the Great War, artists still create work honoring Henry Johnson.

Henry Johnson finally got his Purple Heart in 1996. New York State Governor George Pataki had fought for Henry Johnson's cause. He and many other New Yorkers have tried to make sure that Johnson also gets a Congressional Medal of Honor. The Medal of Honor is this country's greatest military honor. That hasn't happened yet. But Henry Johnson's only surviving son did get to go to a ceremony in Washington, D.C., where his father was finally awarded the Distinguished Service Cross.

Henry Johnson's son Herman Johnson (right) accepts the Distinguished Service Cross on his father's behalf.

Henry Johnson's legacy was felt in another way, too. His son Herman was one of the famed Tuskegee Airmen. The Tuskegee Airmen were a force of African American fighter pilots in World War II. Today, both Harlem's Own and the Tuskegee Airmen are held up as patriots who served their country well. They did so despite the fact that they served in a segregated military. "People didn't think we could fight," remembers Herman. "Now," he says, "people are always talking about the Tuskegee Airmen."

Herman Johnson believes that his father would have been amazed at all the fuss being made about him now. "He didn't expect any laurels," Herman says. Even so, it seems clear that Henry and all of the men of the 369th deserve all the praise and awards and more.

F.9384 NEGRO SOLDIERS DURING WORLD WAR II: BROADSIDE IN COMMENDATION OF HEROIC DEEDS OF NEGROES IN ENCOUNTER WITH GERMAN ARMY. LITHOGRAPH, 1918.

This World War I recruiting poster shows Henry Johnson battling Germans. It is one of the few that showed African American men.

PVT. JOHNSON

"You-all don't want to worry about me. I've been shot before."

The private war of Private Henry Johnson took place in the Argonne Forest in 1918. A member of the Harlem Regiment, Johnson was on watch when his outpost was attacked at night. Bullets drove him to his hands and knees. But still he came up fighting, leaving a trail of destruction half a mile long. He earned the Croix de Guerre — one of France's highest honors.

Join the people who've joined the Army.

This poster of Henry Johnson was used to recruit men in black neighborhoods almost sixty years after he fought so bravely.

Glossary

alliance an agreement between countries to defend one another in case of attack by an enemy force

Allies the countries, including the United States, Great Britain, France, and Russia, that fought the Central Powers in World War I

armistice an agreement to stop fighting that might lead to a peace treaty; a truce

Austro-Hungarian Empire a dual monarchy of Austria and Hungary; it also included territory that later became Czechoslovakia

battalion a military unit made up of three companies; it forms part of a regiment

Central Powers the countries, including Germany, Turkey, and Austria-Hungary, that fought the Allies during World War I

Congressional Medal of Honor the highest military award in the United States, given for bravery

convoy group of ships or vehicles that travel together in the interest of safety

Croix de Guerre French military award given for bravery

division a military unit made up of several regiments

Eastern Front the line of battle in Eastern Europe where the Central Powers fought the Allies

Great Migration the mass movement of African Americans from the South to the North during the first half of the twentieth century

Great War, the World War I

militarism a country's way of developing and supporting strong armed forces to gain power

nationalism a pride and love for one's country and the feeling that it should be strong and the most powerful

no man's land the area between enemy trenches

Purple Heart an award given in the United States to members of the armed forces who have been killed or wounded in action

regiment a military unit made up of three battalions; it forms part of a division

segregation the separation of races

shell-shocked term used to describe the condition of men who lost normal mental functioning as a result of exposure to war

trench a long, narrow ditch with soil piled up on the sides to protect soldiers in combat

trench foot a condition caused by standing too long in wet and cold areas; it can lead to numbness, infection, and gangrene

U-boat an underwater boat, or submarine

Western Front the front line of battle extending from Belgium to the Swiss border, where the Allies (the French, American, and British armies) fought the Central Powers

Index